TOURIST LIBRARY : **28**

JAPANESE COIFFURE

TOURIST LIBRARY

Volumes Already Published

Volumes in preparation

THE JAPANESE-STYLE COIFFURE HARMONIZES
PERFECTLY IN THE LADY'S ENSEMBLE

JAPANESE COIFFURE

BY

R. SAITO, D. LITT.

(Translated by M. G. Mori)

BOARD OF TOURIST INDUSTRY
JAPANESE GOVERNMENT RAILWAYS

EDITORIAL NOTE

It is a common desire among tourists to learn something of the culture of the countries they visit, as well as to see their beautiful scenery. To see is naturally easier than to learn, but flying visits merely for sightseeing furnish neither the time nor opportunity for more than a passing acquaintance with the culture of any foreign people. This is specially true of Japan and her people.

The Board of Tourist Industry recognizes both the obligation and the difficulty of providing foreign tourists with accurate information regarding the various phases of Japan's culture. It is, therefore, endeavouring to meet this obligation, as far as possible, by publishing this series of brochures.

The present series will, when completed, consist of more than a hundred volumes, each dealing with a different subject, but all co-ordinated. By studying the entire series, the foreign student of Japan will gain an adequate knowledge of the unique culture that has evolved in this country through the ages.

For those who wish to follow up these studies with a closer investigation of more erudite works, we sometimes append bibliographies, which we can recommend as authoritative guides for study.

BOARD OF TOURIST INDUSTRY,
JAPANESE GOVERNMENT RAILWAYS.

NOTE

The Japanese Government has adopted a new system
of spelling for certain Romanized Japanese syllable
sounds. Though the spelling has been modified, the
pronunciation remains the same. The modified spelling is given below with the old phonetic spelling in
brackets:

si (shi)		
ti (chi)	tu (tsu)	
hu (fu)		
zi (ji)		
sya (sha)	syu (shu)	syo (sho)
tya (cha)	tyu (chu)	tyo (cho)
zya (ja)	zyu (ju)	zyo (jo)

Naturally, the change has caused the spelling of certain
familiar names of places and things to be altered, for
instance:

Old Spelling	New Spelling
Shinto shrine	Sinto shrine
Chion-in temple	Tion-in temple
Mt. Fuji	Mt. Huzi
Chanoyu	Tyanoyu
Chosen	Tyosen
Jujutsu	Zyuzyutu
Jinrikisha	Zinrikisya

CONTENTS

JAPANESE PERIODS

(in chronological order)

Divine Age (previous to 661 B.C.)

Ancient Period (661 B.C.—592 A.D.)

Nara Period (592—794)

Heian Period (794—1185)

Kamakura Period (1185—1392)

Muromati Period (1392—1568)

Momoyama Period (1568—1600)

Edo Period (1600—1867)

Meizi Period (1867—1912)

Taisyō-Syōwa Period (1912—)

I. UNIQUE AESTHETIC MOTIVES BEHIND JAPANESE STYLES OF HAIRDRESSING

Blessed with a mild climate and an orderly succession of the seasons, with all her mountains and hills clad in verdant foliage and her valleys and plains watered by pure running streams, Japan is indeed a land of superb charm, a veritable paradise of beauty. The dainty flowers that bloom in the spring, the reddening or yellowing of deciduous leaves in the autumn, and other lovely features of natural scenery are inexhaustible in the delight and inspiration they afford. Born and bred in such a country, and nursed amid such scenery, the Japanese people have had their being as a nation for nearly three thousand years. Can it be wondered at, therefore, that they should have a delicate taste for things of beauty, and especially a deep understanding and high appreciation of all forms of art? Their homes, their food and table utensils, their garments, their personal belongings and ornaments, their toilet, their very manners and movements, all express or reflect this accomplished national character. It would indeed appear that they simply cannot tolerate a life devoid of interest and refinement. Even a rustic maiden of lowly birth who "cuts and binds the grass" in the field has enough of the Japanese spirit of poetry in her to derive infinite joy from such wild flowers of autumn as the *hagi* (bush clover) and the *kikyō* (bell-flower). Dwellers in dingy slums hang a tinkling *hūrin* (lit. "wind-bell") from the eaves of their houses, to enjoy its clear melodious sound as it is swayed and rung by each gentle gust of wind ; or adorn their window-ledges with potted plants, or yet again listen with delight to the songs of caged little birds over their verandah. And how much more conspicuous has been this aesthetic or epicurean tendency among people more or less free from the immediate cares and worries of earning a livelihood ! Such men and women have always bestowed the most fastidious attention on their dress and coiffure, so that each article of clothing or style of hairdressing should be so designed as to suit a particular person in his particular station of life, or even on a particular occasion in a particular season of the year. Thus it is that their dress and head-covering have preserved their beauty and appropriateness, qualities which have served to enhance their worth as personal ornaments. That such was already the case in Japan as many as four hundred years ago, is evident from a message sent home by a Spanish missionary who came to this country towards the end of the Muromati period, and who was so wonderstruck at Japanese manners and customs that he reported the women's dress to be of unparalleled beauty and splendour.

But it is in the last three hundred years or so, from the beginning of the Edo period down to the present time, that the art of hair-arrangement has made the most signal progress. It should be remembered that these three centuries have been characterized, generally, by peace at home through all ranks of society, so that the common people have been enabled to enjoy more or less stability of life. There have certainly been small fluctuations of fortune

Young unmarried lady in present-day Japan

accompanying the vicissitudes of social condition, but on the whole both men and women have had enough means and leisure to take sufficient interest in modes of coiffure to adapt them to changing needs, and to devise and make trials of special designs for special occasions. The result has been remarkable progress both from the point of view of aesthetic effect and of technical excellence, and we have not only achieved the full expression of physical beauty but have developed a great variety of styles of hairdressing. Indeed, it would hardly be claiming too much for the Japanese art of arranging the hair to assert that it is something unique in the world. For, after all, it is an expression of the national genius and philosophy of the Japanese people, who believe that each man ought to keep up a life of aesthetic satisfaction to the last moment of his earthly existence.

Maiden in *momo-ware* or
" parted-peach " style

II. BASIC PRINCIPLE: TIED-UP COIFFURE FOR MEN AND PENDANT COIFFURE FOR WOMEN

Since Japanese history extends over two thousand six hundred years, it is not surprising to find that our modes of hairdressing both for men and women have gone through diverse changes. All through the successive periods of this long national career we find, broadly speaking, few examples of either men or women having their hair cut short, for the majority of the people, of both sexes, have always worn their hair dressed or done up in some form or other. And it seems safe to state as a general rule that in all ages previous to the present period (beginning with the Meizi Restoration, 1868), men have had their hair tied up or knotted in some form, while women have worn theirs loosely hanging down their backs. This is obviously due to the different rôles assigned to the sexes in the drama of life. Man's occupation generally demands from him more energetic physical exertion than that of his gentle partner, and his place of work is, as often as not, out of doors. Should emergency summon him, he must go forth to the field of battle where great alacrity is required both in offence and defence. He must either keep his hair trimmed short, or else have it tied or coiled up on his scalp, since long pendant hair would hamper his movements and incapacitate him for active and efficient service. Most women, on the other hand, do not perform strenuous physical labour, but spend much of their time indoors. It is further-

Lady of Nara period, whose coiffure shows ancient Chinese influence
(Photo: K. B. S.)

more considered a woman's duty, her nature-ordained mission, to bestow sufficient care upon her personal appearance to keep herself as pretty as becomes her sex. Since her hair constitutes one of the chief natural ornaments of her person, it is only to be expected that she should prefer to display it to the best advantage by wearing it loosely down her back. Let it be remembered, further, that the Japanese set great store by long, straight or uncurled, raven-black hair, and those who possess such are naturally proud of it; and for a woman to make the most of these features of her hair she has but to let it flow down behind.

Eight to nine hundred years ago Japanese aristocratic culture reached its apogee under the leadership of the Huziwara family. Sitting in palaces, women of noble birth were to be seen dressed in those beautiful costumes which are still regarded as the culmination of the art of personal adornment. They spent their time, day after day and month after month, in poetizing, in appreciating pictures painted by master-artists, or in talking of their amours. These Court ladies actually vied with one another in the sheer length of their hair. They let it hang down the back of their dresses, and as in some instances the hair was one or two feet longer than the lady's height, she would let it trail gracefully behind her on the immaculate floor. If, on the contrary, the hair was short and scanty, she had to make up for the deficiency by means of false hair, known as *kamozi* or *irege*, prepared from other persons' discarded hair. The Huziwara period was indeed the representative age for this fashion in woman's coiffure, which for short may be called the "pendant style." Even

Court ladies of Heian period in pendant coiffure

in that period, however, a different mode or modes of
wearing the hair existed among women in the lower strata
of society, who could not afford to shirk physical labour
if they were to earn their own living or lighten the burden
of their menfolk. They, or many of them, would twist or
plait their hair into a simple knot or coil over the scalp, or
have some of it falling behind the ears, or else keep the
tresses in a bag behind their backs. This mode of hairdressing gradually became more and more national until,
in a subsequent period, we find few women outside the
aristocracy adhering to the flowing style in daily life. Most
women of the people, that is to say, wore their hair knotted in a simple style, which was destined to develop into
more elaborate forms in still later ages. But even in such
classes those who could at all afford or manage it would

make an exception to the general rule and untie their knotted hair to wear it in the time-honoured pendant style when attending the more important ceremonies such as weddings and funerals.

In the Edo period, which immediately preceded the present one (beginning with the Meizi Restoration, 1868), only a very small minority, made up of the Court ladies in Kyōto, adhered to the ancient custom of wearing loose pendant hair. With this negligible exception practically every woman wore her hair in knots, and these knots or chignons became more and more elaborate in design and execution. Even in that age of chignons the wives and daughters of the greater feudal lords or *daimyō,* who were the very aristocrats among aristocrats, wore their hair in what was called the *sage-sitazi,* while some of the numerous women who waited upon those lords and dames in their palaces, or (to be more specific) those who were above a certain rank, had their hair done up in a style called the *kata-hazusi.* The *sage-sitazi* (lit. " ready for the pendant "), the coiffure for *daimyō*'s wives and daughters, was so called because it could be straightway loosened into the pendant coiffure. The *kata-hazusi* (lit. " partly left out "), the style for the maids waiting upon the *daimyō,* consisted of a chignon of which a part was left unfastened to the big and thick bar called a *kōgai* with which the knot was secured. By removing this bar the chignon could at once be undone so that the hair would stream down behind in the regular pendant fashion. All this goes to show that in the upper classes of society in the pre-Meizi periods the pendant coiffure was still considered the proper or basic mode of hairdressing for women. Even

Kata-hazusi, the style for women serving as maids in *daimyō* homes

at the present time ladies privileged to participate in the most important ceremonies at the Imperial Court, such as those connected with enthronement or an Imperial burial, are required to wear their hair loosely in the ancient manner. We see, therefore, that the basic principle of pendant hair for women is still honoured by its observance in exalted circles.

Men at Court, on the other hand, have nearly always worn some form of covering for the head both indoors and out of doors, and irrespectively of social distinctions. This custom, which had existed from very ancient times, lasted until the beginning of the Edo period, that is, until about 350 years ago. When those nobles known as *kuge,* who at the Imperial Court assisted in the government of the country and in the grand ceremonies of State, appeared

Court nobleman in ceremonial dress (Heian period)

there in full dress on such occasions, they wore on their heads what was called a *kanmuri* (lit. "head-covering"*). When dressed in a less formal attire, or even when at home, such a Court noble would change his *kanmuri* for what was called an *ebo* or *ebosi* (lit. "black-cap"). Since there was a fixed or standard pattern for *kanmuri*, these head-coverings were uniform in shape, whereas there was a great variety of styles for *ebosi* suitable to the different classes of people who wore them, ranging from the Court nobles down to the lowliest of men. Those who were in very humble stations of life and could hardly afford the regular *ebosi*, would content themselves with what was called a

---

*The very common translation of this term as "crown" must be here avoided, as the use of a *kanmuri* is not confined to victors or personages endowed with regal power.

Ebosi—less formal than *kanmuri* (from picture-scroll of Kamakura period)

Warrior in *samurai-ebosi* (Muromati period)

hitai-ebosi, which was a triangular piece of black silk cloth or paper secured on to the forehead by means of strings attached to it. This form of headgear still survives in certain rural districts, where it is worn by people taking part in a funeral. In view of its general and popular use we need scarcely be surprised at the very great variety of forms and styles of *ebosi* which gradually came into vogue in response to diverse requirements. Thus we had *tate-ebosi* ("erect *ebosi*"), *naga-ebosi* ("long *ebosi*"), and *ori-ebosi* ("folded *ebosi*") for the upper classes; *samurai-ebosi* for the warrior, and the simple style called *hire* ("plain manners") for the poor and lowly.

As has already been remarked, men in olden times wore some form of headgear or other both in and out of doors and irrespectively of social status. In this sense Japanese head-coverings for men had something in common with ladies' hats in Western countries. Because of this universal and immemorial custom among men their tied-up locks (for so they always kept them) remained invisible under their coverings, so that no necessity or urge was felt to make any effort to adorn their hair. Such a lack of incentive was indeed one important cause of the absence of any progress or change in man's coiffure throughout many centuries. This condition of things persisted until the Momoyama period (400 years ago). Then all men except the numerically negligible aristocratic minority called the *kuge* or Court nobility discarded their headgear and became bare-headed. And that, it should be noted, was the cause why, from that time on, there have followed many and various changes in men's modes or styles of coiffure, changes such as had never been witnessed before.

III. MEN'S COIFFURE IN THE EDO PERIOD

"Sakayaki," a Style Typical of the Age of Warriors

The Asikaga period, which was so called because the Asikagas then monopolized the office of *Syōgun* or Generalissimo, and which lasted about two hundred years ending in 1568, was not, generally speaking, a period of peace and tranquillity. The second half of it was much worse than the first, being characterized by incessant and universal warfare carried on by innumerable war-lords, greater and lesser, who fought one another for territory and power and gloried in their military exploits, giving little thought to peaceful pursuits. In such an age the civil or non-combatant population consisting of farmers, artisans, tradesmen and the rest, maintained a precarious existence amidst the din and glare of battle, in constant fear of death and destruction. In striking contrast to this miserable life of the common people was that of the warrior, who swaggered upon the highways and byways of the country with triumphal pomp. The Asikaga era was thus *par excellence* the age of sworded men. In their everyday life they wore *ebosi*, both at home and out of doors, in accordance with the time-honoured custom; but as soon as they were called out to the field of battle they would change their clothes and buckle on shining armour, discarding their *ebosi* for steel helmets. And as the civil wars increased in intensity and frequency decade after decade until the whole country became a veritable cauldron seething with strife, the peaceful *kanmuri* and *ebosi* were superseded more and more by the warlike helmet; and even when one was enjoying a respite from active service and so wore no helmet, it became customary to avoid *ebosi* and to remain bare-headed, so that one might put on the helmet at a moment's notice. It is true that warriors above a certain rank wore underneath the helmet a sort of *ebosi* called *kabuto-sita* (lit. "under-helmet"); but this privilege was confined to military leaders of the highest class, a small minority, for the great majority of warriors clapped their helmets straight on their bare heads. Now imagine yourself wearing long hair and keeping that heavy metallic covering strapped tight over your scalp for a considerable length of time, and you can easily see that damp warmth about your head would before long become oppressive beyond endurance. Hence the necessity of some contrivance for ventilation, and this need was satisfied by shaving off the forelock. Hair takes time to grow, and it could not regain its former length immediately after the soldier returned home from the campaign to resume his normal life at home. Thus arose the custom of keeping one's forelock shaved all the time, a custom which, originating in an age of unbroken warfare, maintained itself through the succeeding centuries of perfect peace at home, from the Momoyama period to the end of the Edo period. This tonsured portion of the head was called *sakayaki*. Thenceforward, except for the fact that warriors of exalted rank wore *ebosi* on ceremonial occasions of prime importance, all military men were hatless both at home and when attending public offices, and even when taking part in ordinary ceremonies. With his

三玄槍薬

太平姦賊

乱世英雄

大千

一握

福嶋正則公肖像

雄巌便拝書

Shaven-headed and top-knotted warrior in Momoyama period
(Note: Top-knot suspended towards back of head)

~25

forelock shaven off, the *samurai* gathered all the locks that remained around it into a chignon or top-knot (called a *mage*) at the back of his head. This *samurai* fashion in time spread to the common people—farmers, artisans and tradesmen—until every youth became bare-headed, with the fore part of his head clean shaven and a top-knot behind —a curious style of coiffure indeed, which persisted for three hundred years till the beginning of the Meizi period! It means that a vogue arising solely from a wartime exigency and accepted by the whole warrior class finally spread to all the rest of the nation. This explains why the *kuge* or Court nobles, who occupied a position in the country entirely different from that of the sworded gentry and had for a thousand years proudly held their own as a special class, alone persisted in their historic style of hair-dressing and refused to follow the new fashion set by the soldier. They would neither shave off their forelock nor go bare-headed, but still covered their heads with an *ebosi* or *kanmuri*. And there was another exception to the general fashion. Confucian scholars, physicians, and Sintō priests who neither belonged to the common people nor yet had the same social or political status as the *samurai*, followed the nobleman's example in keeping all their locks intact (i.e. without *sakayaki*) and wearing them done up into a special form of coiffure, though they refrained from the use of a *kanmuri* or an *ebosi*. A Sintō priest performing rites before a shrine, however, was always dressed in an ancient costume with a *kanmuri* or *ebosi* on his head. Not a few Confucian scholars and physicians, on the other hand, preferred to have their heads clean shaven, after the well-known manner of Buddhist priests.

Hairdresser busily plying his trade (early Edo period)

Let us now see how the hatless man of the Edo period had his hair done up—the ordinary man, I mean, who belonged either to the military caste or to the commonalty made up of farmers, artisans, and tradesfolk. Going about with his head always exposed, he found that his mode of hairdressing had a direct and important bearing upon his personal appearance as a whole. He realized clearly its effect for better or for worse upon his dignity and his looks. Hence the extra-special care which came to be bestowed upon his coiffure, and the successive and innumerable devices and styles recorded during the two centuries and a half of undisturbed tranquillity. And naturally, as one decade of peace and prosperity followed another, these modes and styles gradually advanced or evolved from the simple to the complex, from the frugal to the luxurious,

Tyasen-mage or " tea-whisk " style of early Edo period

from the unaffected and artless to the elaborate and artificial. The varieties and changes in form and fashion were bewildering.

At the beginning of the Edo period general fashion favoured so broad a *sakayaki* (or tonsure) that the front half of the head was left exposed or hairless. And what little hair remained behind was gathered up into a knob at the back of the head to complete the toilet. There were only two simple methods of making the knot. One was called *tyasen-gami*, because of a fanciful resemblance in shape to the bamboo whisk used in tea ceremony ; it consisted in coiling a piece of string round and round the lower half of the tuft so as to make it stand erect behind. The other was styled *mitu-ori* (lit. "threefold") and consisted in gathering the hair up into a cylindrical shape behind and then bending the upper part of it sharply forward. Even in this latter style, *mitu-ori*, the cylindrical shape was not at all so long as that in later and more developed modes, but was a thick knot far from elaborate in structure.

With but a few special exceptions the fore part of the head was shaven for the *sakayaki*. But in boyhood everyone had only a small tonsured space in the fore part of his crown, so that the forelock itself was left intact. This unshaven forelock was called the *mae-gami* (lit. "front hair or lock"). The part of the forelock immediately above the forehead, however, was so shaved as to make a triangular space with its apex upwards. This unshaven forelock or *mae-gami* was indeed admirably designed to lend a certain charm to one's good looks in childhood.

The times moved even in the placidity of the Tokugawa régime, and brought with them new and varied fash-

Young fan seller with his forelock trimmed in Mid-Edo period
(Wood-block print by Harunobu)

Ityō-mage, which resembles a gingko leaf (By Masanobu)

ions in the shape of the knot, its position (high or low), the form of the *sakayaki* in front of it, and the arrangement of the side-locks on either side of it. Furthermore the styles varied more or less with each class (warriors, farmers, tradesmen and artisans) and locality. Yet, as decades of peace succeeded one another without a break, the ruder modes gradually gave place to the more elaborate and suave styles, a tendency which was the most conspicuous of all among the successive changes of fashion. The "tea-whisk" style already described was in vogue only at the beginning of the Edo period, after which it disappeared completely, so that the other style, *mitu-ori*, enjoyed undisputed popularity. What was more, the *mitu-ori* knot itself became thin and long and straight, and was laid over the shaven fore part of the head as if pressed against it. The knot was no longer *mitu-ori* (threefold) but *hutatu-ori* (doubled). The *sakayaki* became narrower and narrower, and the side-locks correspondingly thicker and broader. With the progress of material civilization certain toilet devices were introduced into the art. One of these was *moto-yui*, a strong but thin cord or string made of paper with which the top-knot was securely tied. Another was a cosmetic paste of solid fat called *kyara-abura* (lit. " aloewood oil"), which helped to mould the knot into good shape and keep it so. There also arose, both in town and country, persons specially trained in hairdressing, and most men now had their hair done up by these experts. All these circumstances combined to bring about new fashions to suit the changing tastes of the customers and the requirements of the times.

It should, however, be noted that down to the Genroku era (1688–1703), which came about the middle of the Edo period, the generality of men and women had preserved, more or less, the sober and thrifty habits reminiscent of the earliest years of the Tokugawa régime; but from that time on the technique of the coiffeur became more and more artificial, until it attained its consummation in the Bunkin style of the Hōreki era (1751–1763), the Honda style of the An'ei and Tenmei eras (1772–1788), and the Ityō style of the Bunka and Bunsei eras (1804–1829). It may indeed be said that these eras together constituted a memorable epoch in the history of Japanese hairdressing.

Though every man normally went bare-headed all through the Edo period, he would cover his head with a cloth cap or hood called a *zukin* (lit. "head-cloth") when going out in the cold and windy days of winter, or when travelling at night. Furthermore, when on a journey men generally wore a broad hat called a *kasa*, which sometimes served as a protection against sunstroke, but was more often useful as a sort of umbrella on rainy days. The shapes and fashions of these hats also varied according as they were worn by the *samurai* or by the plebeian. Among the sworded gentry *ami-gasa* or hats of wicker-work were in general vogue, while the common people as a rule preferred *suge-gasa*, or sedge-hats.

IV. WOMEN'S COIFFURE IN THE EDO PERIOD: PERFECTION IN FORMAL TECHNIQUE

In the Edo period, for the first time in Japanese history, the entire commonalty shared and indulged in the benefits of civilized life. This meant, in other words, that the culture of all the classes whose womenfolk had for a thousand years or more worn their hair in knots instead of in the flowing style of the nobility, had at last attained a degree high enough to enable them to enjoy such conveniences and luxuries. In dress, for instance, their women wore as their outer garment what was known as *kosode* (lit. " little sleeves "), which had till then been worn only as an under-garment by aristocrats. As compared with former periods life in all its aspects had been simplified in the sense that it was free from cumbersome formalities or restrictions. What had hitherto been an article of underwear was now used as an outer garment, and displayed as such it could no longer remain the unostentatious article of clothing it had been as underwear. It came to be adorned with figures or patterns either embroidered or dyed on it which delighted and dazzled the eye with their gorgeous colours and brilliance, and which in due course of time have made the *kimono* one of the glories of Japanese culture. The art of beautifying women's hair naturally made commensurate advances in formal technique. The time was now past when, with all women of the aris-

Burning incense to perfume the hair (early Edo period)

tocracy adhering to the pendant coiffure as the standard style, only their sisters in the lower classes had worn their hair done up in simple knots without thought of formal beauty but merely to ensure freedom of movement. Now that the standard of living had risen considerably in these plebeian classes, and their women went about in full dress or still attended ceremonies with their hair in knots, it was only natural that these knots should have been made more beautiful, and much more skill required in tying them up. Manners and customs, however, do not admit of sudden and drastic changes; and even in the Edo period in its early decades many women still adhered to the traditional flowing coiffure, and such knots as were to be seen in those days were of the simplest form. But as the years went by the coiffeur's technique increased in complexity; and while under the influence of the stereotyping tendencies of the time, it became more formal or conventional, on the other hand it still underwent subtle modifications necessitated by the effort to harmonize the coiffure with the forms and patterns of the dress and the manner of wearing it. This progress kept on year after year, generation after generation, until perfection rendered further advances impossible. It would be a wearisome task now to trace step by step this onward march towards consummation; let us, then, content ourselves with the following summary remark: what had at first been simplicity itself became complex and elaborate after the Genroku era owing to the introduction of *kyara-abura*, the cosmetic of solid fat referred to in our preceding chapter. This pomade enabled the coiffeur to gather all a woman's tresses into one, and to fashion the knob and dispose of the locks around it as

Styles of Kyōto coiffures in late Edo period (By Yamaguti-Soken)

artistically as she pleased. Elaborate and varied methods of marking out and arranging the side-locks and the hindmost lock, and of tying the chignon or main knot (*mage*), were contrived and practised one after another. Different modes and shapes were called into being to suit different occasions and places, persons of diverse ages and stations in life, or even of sundry ranks or positions in the same social stratum or occupation, so that if we were to enumerate all the forms that came into vogue through the successive generations, we should find their number to be legion. Two of them, at least, called respectively the *maru-mage* (lit. "round chignon") and the *simada* (more fully, *simada-mage*, from a proper name), have survived all the vicissitudes of fortune in fashion to our own day.

Let me here mention by way of digression, a special

Perfumed pillow, or aloe pillow, from the aloe-wood incense burnt in it

article of bedding which was in use during the period under review and whose origin and development were intimately connected with the fashionable modes of hairdressing. I refer to the pillow called the *kyara-makura* (lit. "aloe-wood pillow") which was in vogue about the Genroku era. It was a beautiful square wooden pillow adorned with gold-relief lacquer-work and provided with a little drawer in it. The pillow was hollowed out crescent-shaped, which came immediately under the neck, while in the drawer directly underneath it was placed an incense-burner in which to burn some odoriferous wood. Any woman sleeping with her head on this pillow would wake on the morrow to find her tresses fragrantly scented by the ingenious contrivance!

With the growing complexity in the modes of hair-

Comb representing the consummate art of personal adornment

arrangement during the Edo period there appeared in ka-
leidoscopic succession various novel types and styles of
articles and ornaments for the hair, such as combs, bars,
hairpins, and strings and fillets. In fact they were practically innumerable. It is true that the official orders of
prohibition issued from year to year against the use of
articles of luxury were of course applicable to utensils and
trinkets needed in fashionable hairdressing; but by some
excuse or trick invented from a not unnatural desire to own
and use rare things of beauty, women would adorn their
hair with, for example, combs and bars of coral (when
these things were under ban), coolly pretending that the
material was not coral but only *bekkō* or tortoise-shell!
When gold, silver and coral were all taboo, they would
substitute wood as material, but have it most elaborately

and exquisitely carved or ornamented. The illustration (page 39) shows a comb (*kusi*) representative of the extremes to which refinement or the love of rare expensive luxuries was carried in the latter days of the Edo period. The material is coral, which was in those days, by calm falsehood, called tortoise-shell. The entire upper half of the comb including the ridge (or upper edge) is carved to represent a room of the tea-ceremony style, furnished with sliding doors or partitions of ivory which can be moved sideways at will so as to reveal human figures sitting inside in the orthodox manner, painted in low-relief lacquer. The delicacy of design and the skill of execution almost strike a connoisseur dumb with admiration.

Ornamented hairpins (*kanzasi*) were of various materials, such as gold and silver, tortoise-shell, lacquer-ware, and the like. Among the prettiest of hairpins were those with thick clusters of gold and silver blossoms and those that had small silver-coloured strips of paper at the top. Most of such hairpins were worn to adorn the forelock. Then there were others which were shaped like round fans, and still others that looked like the hairy flowers of the *susuki* (pampass grass). Of the strings (*moto-yui*) used in tying the tresses there was at first only one kind, but later on there came into use rather broad hands called *takenaga*, which were of various colours, red, white, among others. This ornamental band (for it was used more as an embellishment than otherwise) was of course a deviation from its original purpose as a substitute for, or a developed form of, the *moto-yui* string. Bands of dappled silk crêpe were also used, and of these again there was a great variety in colour (red, purple, etc.) and form. They served

Kyōto maiden's ornamented chignon

a purpose analogous to that of the ribbon in Western hair-dressing.

Kōgai or bars were made of *taimai* (hawk's-bill tortoise-shell), relief-lacquer ware, and other materials. In some styles either end of the bar could be pulled off from the middle portion, and was decorated with floral figures or family crests. To such a bar was fastened the main knot or *mage*, which was thus held securely in position.

To sum up: everything had become too much ornamented and too artificial in women's coiffure in the latter Edo period. There was formal beauty, to be sure, but little vitality, in it; and, worst of all, it seriously hampered one's active movements. Indeed, it seemed to have reached the highest degree of technical excellence which it was capable of, so that further progress was unthinkable. As a matter of fact, the very times had come to an impasse, which was forced open by the Meizi Restoration, that epoch-making event which breathed new life into the very manners and customs of the nation.

Woman's chignon of Mid-Edo period
with pendant hair

Hairdresser at work (from " Book on Toilet " published in Mid-Edo period)

V. WOMEN'S COIFFURE IN AND SINCE THE MEIZI PERIOD

In the year 2528 of the Japanese National Era, corresponding to 1868 A. D., the government of the country, which had for centuries been entrusted mainly to the military class, was fully and completely restored to the Emperor, who has since then, as in ancient times, ruled the Empire in his own person and capacity. It was the signal for the opening of active intercourse with the leading countries of Europe and America, with which envoys with plenary powers have since been constantly exchanged. The nation's long dream of three centuries thus came to an end, and the scientific civilization of the Occident poured into the country like a flood-tide. These momentous events followed one another like a kaleidoscope at the beginning of the Emperor Meizi's reign, the most memorable ever known since the creation of the Empire. It was only to be expected that the social confusion and changes that came about were most sweeping. Flinging away their custom of tying their locks up into knots, which they had observed in some form or other for two thousand years, men now had their hair cut short, an innovation of no small significance in itself.

Even at such a juncture, when practically the whole nation was bent upon thoroughgoing reforms, it was inevitable that there should nevertheless be a small number of stubborn conservatives, and such die-hards stuck fast to their top-knots while the new fashion of hair-cutting spread like wildfire. The conflict and confusion between old ideas and new were thus evident *on* men's heads as well as *in* them. There was a brief transition period of utter chaos in dress, headgear, footgear, and other personal requisites and, in fact, everything else. After a few years of such turmoil, however, things became more or less settled, and nearly all men now had short hair (often close-cropped or shaved), so that few if any top-knots could be seen. Women's coiffure, in striking contrast to men's, had remained almost unaffected by the general hurricane of innovation, so that it preserved the styles and appearance of the Edo period. And no wonder, for towards the close of that period the art had attained its culmination. Nor would their sex and temperament permit women to follow men's example in revolutionizing their fashions of hair-arrangement. At least for the time being they were content to preserve the styles of their mothers and grandmothers.

In the course of a decade or two, however, women, too, gradually shook off the fetters of certain time-honoured customs and usages, and not only did they appear in fashionable society but they began also to take part in various kinds of work besides their domestic duties. They then found that the traditional modes of hairdressing, exquisite as they were because they represented the most consummate technical skill, were ill-suited to the exacting realities of everyday life in the new age. By what may be called a curious coincidence it happened that about the 19th year of Meizi (1886) the nation's leaders encouraged the Europeanization of all phases of national life, and under

Styles of women's coiffure in Mid-Meizi period

Styles of women's coiffure in Mid-Meizi period

the influence of this Occidentalism, and on the triple ground of health, economy, and convenience, Western styles of hairdressing began to be energetically advocated as preferable to the familiar native modes. The new fashion, first adopted in all classes of the urban population, spread to rural parts, and became generally known as *sokuhatu* (lit. "knotted coiffure"). But to the aesthetic temperament of the Japanese woman, who spends most of her time indoors, primly seated on the *tatami* or matted floor, and who wears no hat of any kind both within and out of doors, the Western mode which consisted in coiling the the forelock into a simple knob was much too inartistic and inelegant to be long endured, although she was by no means insensible of its convenience and its economic and sanitary advantages. To make up for this defect or artistic deficiency, she would sometimes cover her knot with a pretty net on whose silken strings were strung together numerous little beads of red coral ; or she would wear on her head an artificial rose or other flowers ; or yet again adorn the back of her head with a comb of relief-lacquer ware. None of these little devices, however, completely satisfied her taste, with the result that one after another they were totally discarded and forgotten in the course of a few years.

In the 27th year of Meizi (1894) there broke out the Sino-Japanese War, which was continued well into the next year. From the exigencies of wartime economy simple life was strongly advocated, and among the activities of the fair sex those of nurses in the military hospitals attracted special public attention. Now, professional nurses had all along worn their hair in the Western style or *soku-*

Western styles of women's coiffure in fashion in Japan (1885—1887),
when Europeanization went apace under Emperor Meizi

hatu, independently of recent changes in fashion, and the rôle they played in the war paved the way to the revival of the *sokuhatu*. The throne of honour among all the modes of hairdressing which thus came into vogue was occupied by the style known as the *agemaki* (lit. "rolled-up locks"), which was popular with ladies dressed for soirées. The great majority of Japanese women, however, still clung to the traditional methods of hair-arrangement. The *marumage* (lit. "round chignon": already mentioned) was popular with women of middle age, while the *simada-mage* (also already referred to) was preferred by their younger (unmarried) sisters. Other old styles which still retained their popularity were the *ityōgaesi* (fan-shaped knot named from its imaginary resemblance to a leaf of the gingko-tree), *mituwa* (lit. "three loops"), *momo-ware* (lit. "parted peach"), and *tenzin-mage* (named after Sugawara-no-Mitizane, a statesman deified as the incarnation of loyalty to the Emperor).

The Russo-Japanese War, which came ten years later (1904–5), once more plunged the nation into a state of emergency, so that thrift, simplicity and alacrity were required in every phase of its activity. The *sokuhatu* or so-called Western style of coiffure was encouraged through all strata of society. Not only were the times thus favourable to its spread, but in the course of twenty years following its adoption the style itself had undergone technical modifications or improvements along characteristic Japanese lines so as to harmonize very well with the native dress or *kimono*, with the result that what had originally been an Occidental mode of coiffure was now fit to flourish side by side with the traditional styles as a genuine Japa-

Mother (in *maru-mage*) and daughter (with hair hanging) in Mid-Meizi period

nese method of hair-arrangement. One of the improvements referred to consisted in giving the forelock an appearance of amplitude by means of a large pad of false hair placed within it as a sort of frame. Young girls also had this padding for their forelocks, but the rest of their tresses were gathered together behind (with beautifully coloured ribbons tied round them), and hung loosely down the back. This style of coiffure was in great vogue for a time. During the war with Tsarist Russia it became fashionable to wear one's forelock absurdly high, and this style was called the *nihyakusan-kōti*, or " 203-Metre Hill," after the great Japanese victory won in the capture of that salient point at Port Arthur. For a time practically every high-school girl wore her forelock in this manner. This was followed by the opposite practice of pressing and flattening the forelock forwards or outwards, and this was called the *hisasi-gami* after a projecting eave (*hisasi*) to which it was fancifully likened. And, in conformity with the naturalization or Japanization of the Western style of hairdressing, there appeared on the market one after another various utensils and ornaments required in the new style that were well adapted to it and to the native taste as well. There was, for instance, a set of three combs (*sanmai-gusi*) made either of tortoise-shell, metal, or rubber, worn on three sides of the knot (*mage*) so as to encircle it save on one side. Broad ribbons of every colour of the rainbow, from red to purple, could be obtained, and were the delight of young girls. In brief, the whole art of hairdressing in Western style as transplanted on Japanese soil developed along special lines well suited to the *modus vivendi* of the time.

The Meizi period was followed by that of the Emperor Taisyō, which in its turn was succeeded by the present era (Syōwa). During these thirty years the world has witnessed the greatest war in human history, and the invention and rapid development of the aeroplane, wireless telegraphy and radio, all of which have greatly reduced the distance between all the countries on earth as measured in terms of time. East and West now influence each other in daily life as never before in the annals of mankind. At home, moreover, changes in the mode of life have been accelerated by the disastrous earthquake and fire of 1923 (12th year of Taisyō) and other events, so that women have become generally more agile and better fit for work and service on the first line of life's great battle. Their coiffure, accordingly, in unison with all the rest of their

Western style for girls called " 203-Metre Hill "

attire, has become more blithe and sprightly in design and form, influenced as it has been, moreover, by direct contact with the West. Women at the end of the Taisyō era could no longer put up with the style of *sokuhatu* prevalent in pre-earthquake days, in which abundant false hair was inserted not only into the forelock but also into the other parts or locks around it, thus making the whole thing even more cumbersome than the traditional native modes of hair-arrangement. So all false-hair padding has now been done away with, and the protruding forelock known as the *hisasi-gami* has also become a thing of the past. The disappearance of the *hisasi-gami* was followed by a transient fashion called the *mae-ware* (lit. "parted in front"), in which the forelock (no longer containing false-hair stuffing) was divided right in front into two equal halves and pressed down so as almost to overhang the forehead. Shortly afterwards the forelock was parted into two unequal parts in the proporation of 7 to 3, thus giving the new style (still in vogue) the name of *siti-san* ("seven to three"). This was followed by a style known only by the pseudo-English name *ōru-bakku*, that is, "all back," because in this type of coiffure the hair must be all thrown back over the scalp. Generally, however, the appearance of amplitude is obtained by raising the shorter tresses a little way upwards just above the roots instead of bending them all straight backwards; but in the last twelve years or so since the beginning of the present era, marcel waving has also come into vogue. About the 12th or 13th year of Taisyō (1923 or 1924) there was introduced from America, in a fearfully exaggerated form, a style known as *mimi-kakusi* (lit. "hiding the ear"), the technique of which consisted in adding

Girl of early Taisyō Era with her hair parted in front

a little false hair to the side-locks and lowering them so far down as to hide the ears with them. It was such an extreme freak of fashion that it did not last more than a few years. About that time a small minority, ever athirst for the bizarre in fashion bobbed their hair, but the bob has never gained enough votaries here to entitle it to the name of a fashion. In the last two or three years a few women with bobbed hair have been seen with "permanent waves" in their locks, but this style is not likely to be widely accepted as being well suited to Japanese national character. There was also a style of chignon called *yukue-humei* (lit. "missing" or "whereabouts unknown") in which all the ends of the tresses were concealed within the ample knot; but it proved only a short-lived caprice. In the last six or seven years women's hair-knots have gene-rally been lowered in position and reduced in size; but it is doubtful whether these low and small chignons will long enjoy popularity as being in complete harmony with the native dress. Hairdressers nowadays design new forms for each New Year, for summer wear, or to commemorate current events of importance; but they are nearly all e-phemeral in character, only a very few, if any at all, sur-viving their immediate occasions or purposes. What a striking contrast to these are the *maru-mage* and *simada*, purely Japanese styles which have outlived the test of years, and which, though lacking in mobile expression, are likely to endure for many years more.

VI. PRESENT-DAY STYLES OF COIFFURE

(I) Pure Japanese Modes

It has already been shown that the purely native styles of hairdressing had attained, in the course of more than two hundred years of the Edo period, a state of perfection which admitted of only very slight additional modifications. Such variations, required only to suit different circumstances and occasions, were of a character scarcely to be noticed by anyone without an expert's discernment. They consisted, for example, in slightly heightening or lowering the forelock, increasing or reducing the swelling or amplitude of the side-locks or of the padding within them, or almost imperceptibly altering the position or shape of the main knot (*mage*). We may say that these little modifications left the form of each style essentially unchanged, so mellow a stage of progress had the traditional art of the hairdresser reached by the end of the Edo period. But until the beginning of the Meizi period their recognized styles or patterns were very numerous. There were in fact scores of them. Since then, by a sort of natural selection, many species of them have disappeared one by one, until only a few of them, viz. the *maru-mage, simada, ityō-gaesi,* and *momo-ware,* survive today. These few survivors, which time's severe test has proved to be the fittest, have secured for themselves a position of pride as styles of hairdressing symbolic of Japan. And of all these styles the most pre-eminently Japanese in the best sense are the *simada* and *maru-mage*, which are indispensable in completing the dignified appearance of a lady in full dress *à la japonaise*.

Simada-mage. Of the existing styles of coiffure which are genuinely Japanese, that which strikes one as the most beautiful and gorgeous is the *simada-mage*, which is most appropriate for young girls in the flower of maidenhood. What may be regarded as a primitive form or prototype of *simada-mage* appears represented in the heads of clay images unearthed from tombs which are believed to be a thousand years old, so that this style must be said to have a history of ten centuries behind it. Even the present form of technical perfection is at least a hundred and fifty years old. In view of this long record it is not surprising that the term *simada-mage* should have included more than a dozen varieties of the style in pre-Meizi days. Even at the present time there are three or four sub-styles, namely, *taka-simada* ("high *simada*"), ordinary *simada*, *tubusi-simada* ("pressed-down *simada*"), and *yui-wata* (lit. "tied cotton").

Of these the *taka-simada* is the most representative type of *simada*, and indeed by far the noblest of all indigenous styles of coiffure. Of course it best becomes young ladies between sixteen and twenty years of age, and indispensable to them on that most important ceremonial occasion of their lives, the wedding. It is a highly significant fact about this style that it is considered taboo for married women, being sacred to virginity. One must of course have one's hair done in this style by an expert, for only an expert can do it. To begin with, all the locks (fore-

Taka-simada or "high *simada*" (most ornate style of coiffure)

Yui-wata—a kind of *simada-mage*   (Photo: M. Horino)

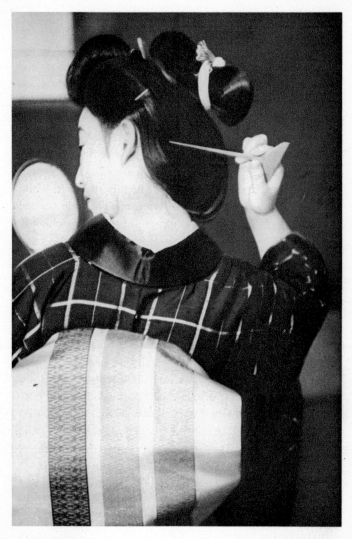

Tubusi-simada or "pressed-down *simada*"   (Photo: Nippon Kōbō)

lock, side-locks, and back hair) must be moulded into
suitable shape by means of a cosmetic paste of rather hard
fat. The hairdresser then proceeds to the making of the
knot or *mage*. In order to give the knot the desired
shape, thick dark-blue paper called *kondosa* is pasted on
to the interior side of it, thus making it more stable and
thereby rendering manipulation easier. The side-locks are
made to appear as ample as possible, and the knot is greatly elevated (say, an inch and a half) ; hence its name *taka-
simada* or *taka-mage*, that is, "high *simada* or chignon."
The chignon-band or *negake* used in this style is a white
or silver-coloured fillet called *takenaga*. The string called
hane-motoyui with which the uppermost part of the chignon
is tied is white on ordinary occasions ; but on the most
formal occasions golden and silver strings should be used
instead. For hair-ornaments combs and hairpins are required, the hairpins (*kanzasi*) being of two kinds : those
stuck in from the front and those inserted in the back.
The combs are usually of raised-lacquer work, while the
ornamental front hairpins are generally fanciful represen-
tations of flowers, and the back hairpins, of beaten silver.
As a rule no bar or *kōgai* is used in this style ; but for a
bride in full wedding costume a tortoise-shell bar of considerable size is inserted at the bottom of the knot. At
both ends of this bar are engraved *syō-tiku-bai* ("pine,
bamboo and plum"), *turu-kame* ("cranes and turtles,"
symbols of long life), and other objects popularly regarded
as auspicious signs or omens. Combs and hairpins must
also be all of spotless tortoise-shell of a pale yellow hue,
since all other materials, such as metal, are considered
absolutely inappropriate. To complete the bride's hair-

Ordinary *simada*   (Photo: M. Horino)

dressing, a broad band of white cloth with crimson lining called *tuno-kakusi* (lit. "covering for the horns"), is wound around the front half of the head. The total impression thus created is one of great beauty and nobility.

The ordinary *simada* style, as distinguished from the *taka-simada* just described, is not so high as the latter, nor is it so exclusively ceremonial in function. As for the *tubusi-simada* ("pressed-down *simada*"), it is even simpler and homelier than either. The part of the knot a few inches above the base is tied securely down to the base by means of a string so as to give the whole knot a somewhat flattened appearance. This style is regarded as suitable to women in gay quarters, and to others who follow them in taste and fashion, so that it is particularly favoured by *geisya* but avoided in households with austere and refined taste. Since it is even more informal or less ceremonial than the ordinary *simada*, one who has her hair done in *tubusi-simada* enjoys great freedom in the choice of combs and hairpins, so that she can depend on her own individual taste and discretion as her chief guide.

Maru-mage. Best suited to married women, this mode of coiffure is traceable to what was known at the beginning of the Edo period as the *katuyama* style, which underwent a long process of gradual improvement or refinement until, about a hundred and fifty years ago, it attained almost the identical form that it bears at the present day. There have been, to be sure, more or less modifications (of a brief duration) in the size and shape of its various parts, such as the forelock, the side-locks and the back hair; but as a whole the style has preserved the same definite contour in the last century and a half. In

Maru-mage or " round chignon " (chiefly for married women)

pre-Meizi days it had its votaries mostly in Eastern Japan with Edo as its centre, and was not much in evidence in Kyōto and the provinces west of it. Today, on the contrary, it ranks as the most representative of all native Japanese styles of hairdressing throughout the whole Empire. In view of its virtual monopoly by married women as a symbol of wifehood, it is never usurped by their unmarried sisters. But this negative rule has one exception. Women serving as waitresses in certain high-class restaurants, no matter whether they are married or not, have their hair done in *maru-mage* upon reaching a certain age. But there are *maru-mage's* and *maru-mage's*! The style that suits this class of women is intended to appeal to *their* idea of what is exquisite in fashion, while the mode which is acceptable to ladies aims chiefly at nobility of design and form. Naturally the two modes differ a little in the position of the knot, as well as in the size and shape of the locks around it.

As with the *simada* so with the *maru-mage*, the coiffeur begins by applying the cosmetic paste of fat to the forelock, the side-locks and the back hair so as to mould them into desired form. She (for a hairdresser for women is always a woman) then proceeds to the making of the *mage* or knot. A *maru-mage* knot, unlike that of the *simada*, consists of hair (often including much false hair) wound round a frame called a *mage-gata*, a kidney-shaped bag or pad of dark-blue paper stuffed with cotton and coated with a cosmetic paste immediately before it is used. The part of the hair immediately below the framed knot is wound securely around with a white cord of tough paper ; but usually a string of beads (of coral, chrysoprase, gold

Middle-aged lady in *maru-mage* practising tea ceremony

or silver) is used in addition for ornamental purposes. The inner side and the two ends (or right and left sides) of the kidney-shaped knob or *mage* are covered and adorned by a piece of cloth called *tegara-gake*. It varies in colour and material according to age and occasion. The most usual colours are crimson, purple, blue, and white, and each colour may vary in intensity or hue. In all cases the material is either dappled silk crêpe or *habutae* (fine soft silk), and both are very beautiful indeed when so used. As in the *simada*, combs, bars, and hairpins used in the *maru-mage* should be of spotless tortoise-shell for ceremonial occasions, but for most other occasions one may use spotted tortoise-shell, raised-lacquer ware, gold or silver, precious stones, or any other substance, in fact, that suits one's taste or inclination. Here, then, one enjoys freedom of choice among a wide variety of materials.

Since a woman may begin wearing her hair in this style immediately after marriage and keep it up until old age, if she so wills, the *maru-mage* can serve her a very long time indeed, though its chignon, etc. may change slightly in size or shape according to age and fashion. From this point of view, as well as from other considerations, the *maru-mage* seems justly entitled to be honoured as the best representative of all native Japanese styles of hair-arrangement.

Momo-ware. This is for girls from thirteen to eighteen years of age. The name, as already mentioned, literally means "a peach cut in two," and comes from the shape of the chignon or *mage*. It is adorned with a comb having an artificial flower on the upper edge of it, or with a hairpin also decorated with an artificial flower or flowers. The

Momo-ware or " parted peach " (for young maidens only)

Two young *geisya* in a kind of *momo-ware*

Girl in *momo-ware* practising flower-arrangement   (Photo : K.B.S.)

style is not only dignified but makes one look at once pretty and sweet. As girls between thirteen aud eighteen nowadays attend high schools (i.e. secondary schools corresponding to "middle schools" for boys), they prefer the lighter Western styles of coiffure to the *momo-ware*, the style suited to their age, so that in ordinary families few girls are seen with their hair done in this native fashion. It is, however, still the invariable mode among very young dancing girls known in Tōkyō as *hangyoku*, or as someone has humorously called them, "embryonic *geisya*."

Ityō-gaesi. Next to the *simada* and *maru-mage*, this is the native Japanese style that is most in vogue at present. Unlike the *momo-ware*, it is the style for middle-aged women, but it is so informal that it is never admitted into a refined or austere family. It is the favourite mode of hair-arrangement with waitresses in restaurants and married women in the lower classes. The forelock, the side-locks and the back hair are, roughly speaking, of the same form as those of the *maru-mage* and *simada*, but the *mage* or chignon may be described as resembling an S or the figure 8 made to lie down on its side. It is rather low or flat compared with the knob of either *simada* or *maru-mage*. No cloth is attached to it for embellishment, and the combs and hairpins are most informal, so that one enjoys entire freedom of choice in these matters. Like the *maru-mage*, the *ityō-gaesi* was mainly confined to Edo and the surrounding provinces in Tokugawa days, being little in evidence in Western Japan, but today it enjoys a nationwide vogue.

Other Indigenous Styles. First among these should be mentioned the *osage*. It is the pendant style in which

Ityō-gaesi (supposedly resembling a gingko leaf)

~73

a lady in exalted circles—a princess, a peeress, or the wife or daughter of a high official—has her hair done when attending a wedding or a grand ceremony at the Imperial Court. On such an occasion she must be dressed in the ancient style of ceremonial dress called *koutigi-hakama*. This form of loose coiffure is not an exact reproduction of the ancient pattern, yet it is certainly modelled upon it. By its very nature, however, it has little or nothing to do with the current customs and fashions of the majority. Among the more popular or plebeian forms of coiffure not already mentioned are the *mituwa* (lit. "triple loop"), *katura-sitazi* and the extremely informal *kusimaki* (lit. "coiled round the comb"), all of which are fast losing their votaries.

(2) Naturalized Foreign Styles

Since the native Japanese styles of hairdressing are all perfected and mature patterns, they admit of only imperceptible modifications which are not allowed to change the total impressions given by those patterns. On the other hand, imported Western styles, though more or less naturalized, have not yet prescribed for themselves definite limits of formal development. Moreover, new waves of fashion emanating from America and Europe continually beat upon these shores year after year, causing at times rather violent fluctuations in our modes of hairdressing along exotic lines. We have already, in our preceding chapter, traced the outlines of these changes and freaks of fashion. Let us, then, confine ourselves to the description of two styles of Western hairdressing that have been, so to speak, carrying all before them since the outbreak of the present China affair. Both are simple and informal,

Current mode of hairdressing in Western style

Latest mode of hairdressing in Western style

Latest mode of Western hairdressing in Japan   (Photo: M. Horino)

light and free in appearance, appropriate to the emergency that confronts the nation and her unshaken determination to live fully and bravely up to it.

The forelock (in the first style) is parted in the proportion of seven to three. The hair is left entirely waveless or waved ever so slightly. All the tresses are combed boldly backwards so as to be gathered together into a little chignon of some form or other well at the back of the head. The knot varies in shape almost from person to person according to individual likes and dislikes, so that it may be slightly elongated from side to side, or nearly spherical, or assume diverse other forms. There is no need of combs, hairpins or ribbons for decorative purposes. In fact, its extreme informality and naïveté are such as to remind one of the wileless and frugal methods of hair-arrangement in vogue at the beginning of the Edo period. By dispensing altogether with any sort of ornament it has freed itself from all taint of affectation, and it well becomes almost any type of face, oval, longish, or square, whose natural beauty it helps to reveal to the best advantage by its very simplicity. Yet a word of criticism here seems called for. How can we pretend that the position of the chignon, right at the extreme back of the head, symbolizes the rise of Japan like the morning sun above the eastern bars? It is certainly a question how long this fashion will last.

The other Western style now in fashion also requires all the tresses to be combed down to the back of the head just above the nape of the neck, but there the end of the tresses thus gathered together is gently curled upwards instead of being made into a knot. This curling up may be done either by the hairdresser's sheer dexterity or by means of permanent waving. This is nothing more or less than an adaptation by young Japanese women, under the stimulating influence of the present emergency, of a style of coiffure that was in vogue in Europe several years ago. It resembles the other Western style, described in the previous paragraph, in requiring absolutely no ornament of any kind. It is simplicity itself.

There are numerous other styles of hairdressing *à l' occidentale* that are favoured or preferred by women with idiosyncracies in tonsorial taste, but none of them has had enongh followers to produce any discernible effect on fashion, or to deserve a paragraph to itself in this brief survey.

Simada-mage, woman's chignon, of Mid-Edo period

VII.   HAIRDRESSING AND CLOTHING :   A STUDY IN SYMMETRICAL BEAUTY

Hairdressing owes its origins and evolution to man's desire and effort to improve his personal appearance, and this is still more true of his fair partner on the pilgrimage of life.   Since the head is a part of the human body, it cannot be made beautiful by treating it as if it were independent of the rest.   In architecture, in landscape gardening, in interior decoration, in the art of dress-designing, and in everything else, the Japanese have always paid special attention to the problem of harmony and balance with the surroundings and the background ; and indeed they have always shown superior talent and ability to achieve the desired end.   It is only to be expected then that this artistic genius should never fail to seek and exhibit beauty of symmetry between forms of coiffure and styles of dress, no less than between other aspects of personal appearance or toilet.   Of course every fashion and every style may not have been conceived and designed in conscious obedience to this artistic principle or tendency, but it is at least significant to observe that the successive changes and variations in styles of hairdressing have always been made more or less in step with the current modes of dress as to design, colour, tailoring and the manner of wearing it, there being considerable latitude of choice and taste in all these matters.

Warrior (Kabuki actor) in shoulder-cloth (*kataginu*)
and pleated skirt (*hakama*)

Girls in gay quarters at end of Edo period

Let us begin with men's attire. Reference was made in an early chapter to the headgear for men called the *kanmuri* and *ebosi*, neither of which had any brim or other lateral protrusion to speak of. When these coverings were in vogue, men's clothes (whether called *nōsi, kariginu,* or *sitatare*) were generally very large and loose, with extremely broad and flowing sleeves ; and as very stiff fabrics were chosen for material, they gave one the appearance of being broad-shouldered and masculine. The extreme in this direction was represented by costumes known as *kowa-syōzoku,* i.e. "stiff costumes." Of these the *kariginu* (" hunting costume ") served best to give prominence to the square shoulders because the upper part of the sleeves is deliberately left unstitched so as to expose the underwear just at the shoulders. Now all these devices were intended to counterbalance the impression of a very small head created by the brimless *kanmuri* or *ebosi,* an impression that would otherwise contrast too sharply with the rich beauty of the remaining or lower half of the body. We see the same idea in operation even more conspicuously in the costume (called *kami-simo*) of the bare-headed and top-knotted man in the Edo period. The stiff sleeveless coat or shoulder-cloth (*kata-ginu*) worn by him on ordinary ceremonial occasions was broadest at the top, where it formed a straight and sharp ridge either end of which projected considerably beyond the shoulder-blade. This shoulder-cloth (which by the way covered the entire back but left the front open) was well adapted to give due dignity to the upper part of the body by relieving the feeling of barrenness or scantiness caused by the uncovered head. An example of the contrary tendency is furnished

by the current ceremonial costume of the Japanese gentle-
man known as *haori-hakama*, which consists of a coat
(*haori*) and a pleated skirt (*hakama*). It certainly gives
one an impression of stable equilibrium, but it lacks symmetrical beauty because the figure of the man wearing it
is broadest at the base. It is, after all, a product of the
transition period, and we may confidently expect further
developments in the future.

Our next, or last, business is to consider women's hair
in relation to their dress. At the beginning of the Edo
period, when they did their hair in the simplest of styles,
they wore clothes with very large and showy figured patterns, the centre or most important part of which was lo-
cated high up over and around the shoulders. This device
admirably served not only to counteract the over-simplicity of their coiffure but to give the necessary prominence
to that most important portion of the human body, the
breast, and add beauty to the face. As generation succeeded generation, however, there were (owing to complex
causes) fewer and fewer women clad in *kimono* decorated
all over with floral and other designs, and the position and
the centre of such designs as still remained were greatly
lowered. The *obi* or sash, on the contrary, gradually became broader and more gorgeous, and the later manner of
tying it was so elaborate that it gave the sash very considerable prominence. But the part of the dress visible above
the *obi* was now left almost without designs or figures, so
that it became quite plain and uninteresting. This may
indeed be regarded as one of the prime motives for the
richly embellished styles of hairdressing that came into
vogue notably in the second half of the Edo period. The

Bride in *taka-simada*

reader is once more reminded of the inordinate extension or protrusion of the side-locks and the back hair, the enlargement of the chignon (*mage*), combs and bars and hairpins of precious metals, tortoise-shell, coral, or what-not, all of fine workmanship, and ribbons or bands of red and purple cloth. It was by such means that beauty of symmetry was sought. As representing the extreme to which this effort at symmetrical beauty was carried we must mention the coiffure of gay women called *oiran* who flourished in Yosiwara and elsewhere during the Edo period. In that style the chignon was done up into a *hyōgo-mage* or a *simada-mage* in an absurdly exaggerated form by the help of false hair called *syaguma*, while a large number of combs, bars and hairpins of various descriptions were employed for ornamental purposes, supplemented by golden and silver strings and fillets. The head, in short, was gorgeousness itself. No less gorgeous was the long over-dress called an *utikake*, the lower end of which was particularly beautiful. This trailing skirt, at the lower end where the lining was turned outwards, was from four to seven inches thick. Altogether five to seven skirts were there visible one above the other, like so many thick hoops of diverse colours, encircling the foot of the dress. The great splendour of the *oiran's coiffure de luxe* previously mentioned was evidently deemed necessary to maintain a symmetrical balance with the lower half of the body so richly attired.

Coming back to our own time, we find symmetry in costume perfectly maintained by a young lady in full dress, with her beautifully figured and extremely broad flowing sleeves (*huri-sode*). As for those who wear their hair in Western style, they make amends for its over-simplicity

Geisya in informal *simada*   (Photo: Nippon Kōbō)

and dryness by putting on *kimono* with very large and gorgeous patterns on them, whose centre, moreover, is high up compared with former days. In this respect the fashion bears close resemblance to that which obtained at the beginning of the Edo period. And yet, after all, such symmetry as we have observed always to exist between coiffure and dress is, probably, more instinctively than consciously achieved by the artistic temperament of the nation. For life in Japan is impossible and unimaginable apart from efforts (deliberate or subconscious) to give concrete expression to Beauty. This, be it said, is as true of the Japanese art of hairdressing as of any other field of life and activity in this sun-kissed land of green hills and crystalline rills.

A typical country maiden
in Sado Island

JAPANESE COIFFURE

日 本 人 ノ 髮 容

昭和十四年四月二十五日印刷　國際觀光局
昭和十四年四月三十日發行

　　　　　　　東京市麴町區丸ノ内一丁目
發 行 兼　　　財團
印 刷 者　　　法人 國際觀光協會

　　　　　　　宮 部 幸 三

　　　　　　　東京市牛込區榎町七番地
印 刷 所　　　大日本印刷株式會社
　　　　　　　榎 町 工 場

　　　　　　　丸 善 株 式 會 社
發 賣 所　　　東京市日本橋區通二丁目
SELLING　　　MARUZEN CO. LTD., TOKYO
AGENTS　　　ジヤパン・ツーリスト・ビューロー
　　　　　　　（日 本 旅 行 協 會）

　　　　　　　JAPAN TOURIST BUREAU
　　　　　　　TOKYO

定 價 金 五 拾 錢

(239 L 28-2039)